Contents

AGES 10–11
KEY STAGE 2

Premier

Place value

To **multiply** by 100, move all the digits two places to the left.

To **multiply** by 1000, move all the digits three places to the left.

			3	6	.	4
	3	6	4	0	.	
3	6	4	0	0	.	

To **divide** by 100, move all the digits two places to the right.

To **divide** by 1000 move all the digits three places to the right.

4	1	3	0	.		
	4	1	.	3	0	
		4	.	1	3	0

I

Multiply each of these by 100.

a 745 → ⬚

  5610 → ⬚

  8.65 → ⬚

  298 → ⬚

  3114 → ⬚

  21.8 → ⬚

Multiply each of these by 1000.

b 26 → ⬚

  968 → ⬚

  6.05 → ⬚

  0.003 → ⬚

  314 → ⬚

  2317 → ⬚

  19.8 → ⬚

  1.65 → ⬚

Divide each of these by 100.

c 4800 → ⬚

  27 300 → ⬚

  4910 → ⬚

  62 100 → ⬚

  38 000 → ⬚

  3158 → ⬚

Divide each of these by 1000.

d 294 000 → ⬚

  6 148 000 → ⬚

  81 500 → ⬚

  62 → ⬚

  817 000 → ⬚

  1 722 000 → ⬚

  13 100 → ⬚

  40 → ⬚

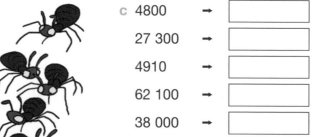
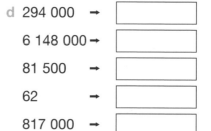
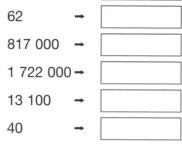

II

Write the missing numbers.

a 48 × ◯ = 4800

b ◯ × 1000 = 570

c 387 ÷ 100 = ◯

d ◯ ÷ 100 = 0.06

e 61.3 × ◯ = 61300

f ◯ ÷ 1000 = 8.5

g 0.07 × ◯ = 7

h ◯ ÷ 10 = 16.05

i ◯ × 100 = 9413

Number sequences

Look at the difference between numbers in a sequence.

This can show the **pattern** or **rule**.

17 20 23 26 ...

The rule is +3

9 4 −1 −6 ...

The rule is −5

I Continue these sequences and write the rules.

a | 7 | 11 | 15 | 19 | | | |

Rule: _____

b | 23 | 15 | 7 | −1 | | | |

Rule: _____

c | 7.5 | 9 | 10.5 | 12 | | | |

Rule: _____

Write the missing numbers in these sequences.

d | 6 | | 28 | 39 | | |

e | 0.9 | 0.89 | | | 0.86 | |

f | 55 | 40 | | | | −20 |

g | 37 | | | | 73 | 82 |

h | 0.25 | 0.5 | | | | 1.5 |

i | | | −63 | −44 | −25 | |

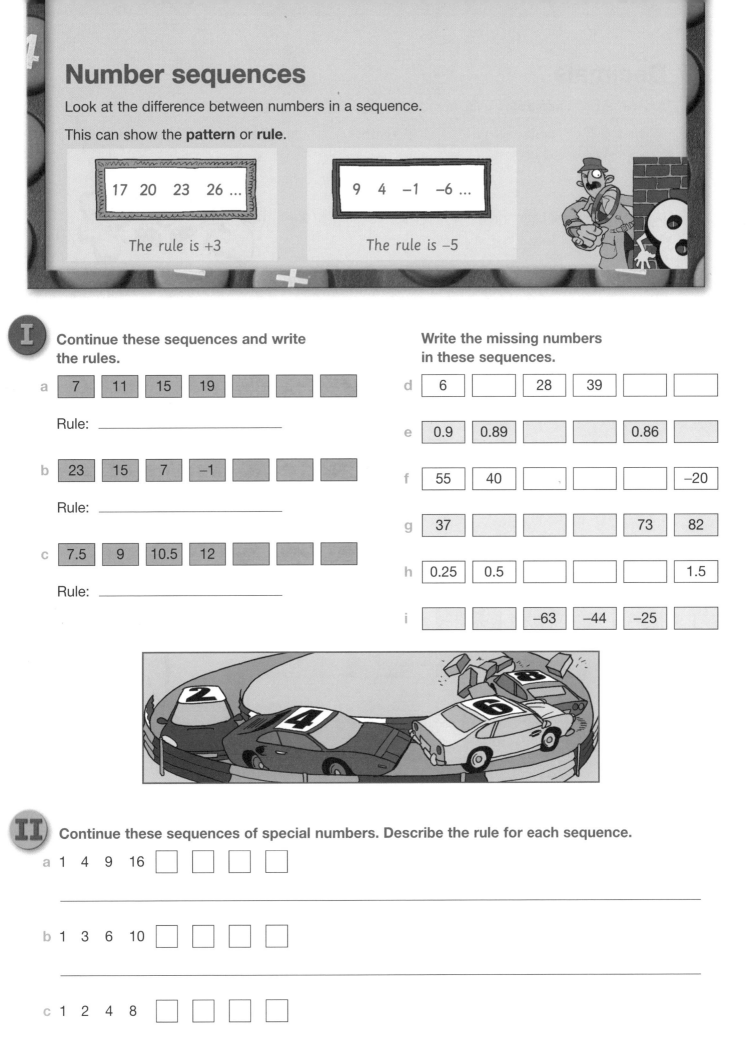

II Continue these sequences of special numbers. Describe the rule for each sequence.

a 1 4 9 16 ☐ ☐ ☐ ☐

_____

b 1 3 6 10 ☐ ☐ ☐ ☐

_____

c 1 2 4 8 ☐ ☐ ☐ ☐

_____

Decimals

A decimal point **separates** units from tenths.

tens	units		tenths	hundredths	thousandths
1	7	.	8	3	5

In seventeen point eight three five, the value of the digit 3 is 3 hundredths or → $\frac{3}{100}$

I Complete these.

Write the value of the red digit.

a 87.384 → [   ]

b 4.006 → [   ]

c 13.45 → [   ]

d 117.805 → [   ]

e 3.068 → [   ]

f 20.309 → [   ]

Continue these patterns for two more numbers.

g [1.96] → [1.97] → [1.98] → [   ] → [   ]

h [3.018] → [3.019] → [3.02] → [   ] → [   ]

i [4.947] → [4.948] → [4.949] → [   ] → [   ]

j [0.998] → [0.999] → [1.0] → [   ] → [   ]

II Rearrange each set to make a decimal number as near as possible to 1. There must be one number in front of the decimal point e.g. 6.401.

a

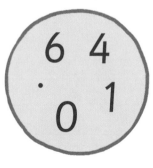

6 4 . 0 1 0

b

2 7 . 1 4 1

c

0 0 1 . 4

d

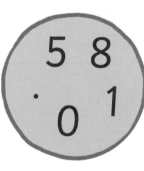

5 8 . 0 1

[   ]   [   ]   [   ]   [   ]

4

Multiples

Multiples are numbers made by **multiplying together** two numbers.

12, 90, 240 and 3000 are all multiples of 3. These numbers are divisible by 3.

Learn and use these rules of divisibility.

A whole number is a multiple of:

2 if the last digit is even e.g. 752

3 if the sum of its digits can be divided by 3 e.g. 132 (1 + 3 + 2 = 6)

4 if the last two digits can be divided by 4 e.g. 528 (28 is divisible by 4)

5 if the last digit is 5 or 0

6 if it is even and divisible by 3, e.g. 156

10 if the last digit is 0

I Look at these numbers.

| 296 | 4120 | 930 | 2004 | 825 | 726 |

a Which numbers are multiples of 3? _____

b Which numbers are divisible by 4? _____

c Which number is a multiple of both 4 and 6? _____

d Which numbers are divisible by both 3 and 5? _____

e Write each of the numbers on the Venn diagram.

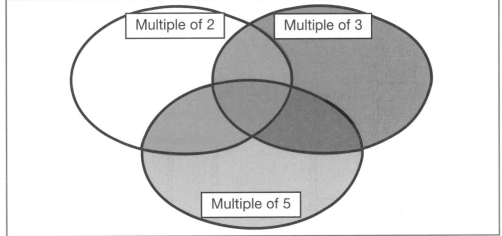

II 504 is divisible by many numbers. Answer these.

a Tick the numbers below that 504 is exactly divisible by.

2 ☐   3 ☐   4 ☐   5 ☐   6 ☐   7 ☐   8 ☐   9 ☐   10 ☐

b Find another number that is divisible by more than six of these numbers. _____

c What is the smallest number that is divisible by 2, 3, 4 and 5? _____

Ratio

Ratios are used to **compare the number of parts** that make up a whole quantity.

In this flower border there are two tulips for every one daffodil.

The ratio of daffodils to tulips is 1 for every 2, written as 1:2.

I Write the ratio of rectangle to square bricks for each garden path design.

a

Ratio [ ]

b

Ratio [ ]

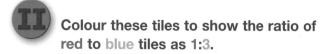

c

Ratio [ ]

d If 48 square bricks are used for each design, how many rectangle bricks are needed for each?

Design **a** [ ]

Design **b** [ ]

Design **c** [ ]

II Colour these tiles to show the ratio of red to blue tiles as 1:3.

a

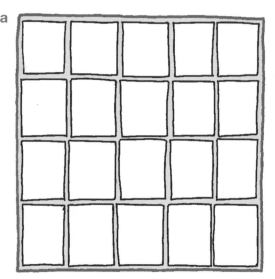

Colour these tiles to show the ratio of green to yellow tiles as 1:4.

b

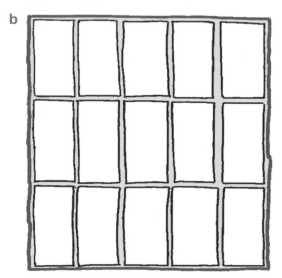

Quadrilaterals

Shapes with four straight sides are called quadrilaterals.

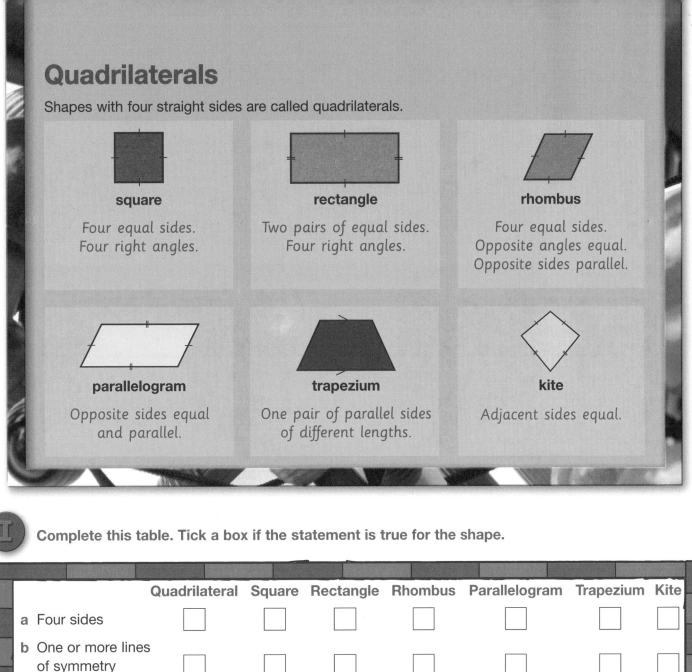

square
Four equal sides.
Four right angles.

rectangle
Two pairs of equal sides.
Four right angles.

rhombus
Four equal sides.
Opposite angles equal.
Opposite sides parallel.

parallelogram
Opposite sides equal
and parallel.

trapezium
One pair of parallel sides
of different lengths.

kite
Adjacent sides equal.

I Complete this table. Tick a box if the statement is true for the shape.

	Quadrilateral	Square	Rectangle	Rhombus	Parallelogram	Trapezium	Kite
a Four sides	☐	☐	☐	☐	☐	☐	☐
b One or more lines of symmetry	☐	☐	☐	☐	☐	☐	☐
c Opposite sides same length	☐	☐	☐	☐	☐	☐	☐
d Adjacent sides same length	☐	☐	☐	☐	☐	☐	☐
e Both pairs of opposite sides parallel	☐	☐	☐	☐	☐	☐	☐
f One or more right angles	☐	☐	☐	☐	☐	☐	☐

II Draw two different quadrilaterals on the grid with a ruler.

They must each have the following:

• fewer than 2 right angles

• opposite sides equal

• opposite sides parallel.

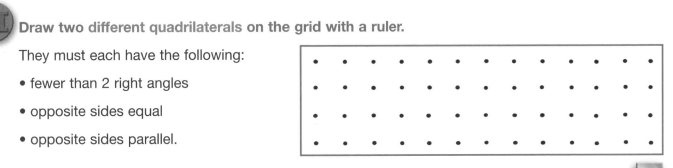

Comparing and ordering decimals

When you put decimals in order, look carefully at the value of each digit.

It may help to write the numbers in a column lining up the decimal point.

> means 'is greater than'	
4.85 > 4.588	
< means 'is less than'	
3.07 < 3.71	

```
1 0 . 6 5
    8 . 9
    8 . 7 2
    8 . 0 5 5
```
Compare each column, starting from the left.

I **Look at these numbers.**

6.93	6.59	6.095	6.05	6.198	6.85	6.9	6.625

a Put them in order, starting with the smallest.

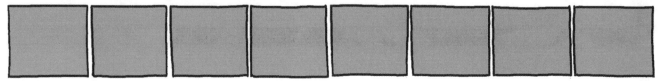

Choose any number from the list above to complete these.

b 7.04 > [ ] > 6.92

c 6.9 > [ ] > 6.63

d 6.79 < [ ] < 6.89

e [ ] < 6.82 < [ ]

f [ ] > 6.4 > [ ]

g [ ] < 6.19 < [ ]

II **Now try this.**

Use the digits 1, 2, 6, 9 and a decimal point.

[ ] . [ ] [ ] [ ]

a Make six numbers between 0 and 2. Write them in order, starting with the smallest.

[ ] [ ] [ ] [ ] [ ] [ ]

b Make six numbers between 9 and 10. Write them in order, starting with the smallest.

[ ] [ ] [ ] [ ] [ ] [ ]

Use this area to show your working out.

Mental addition and subtraction

Use mental methods to **add** and **subtract**.

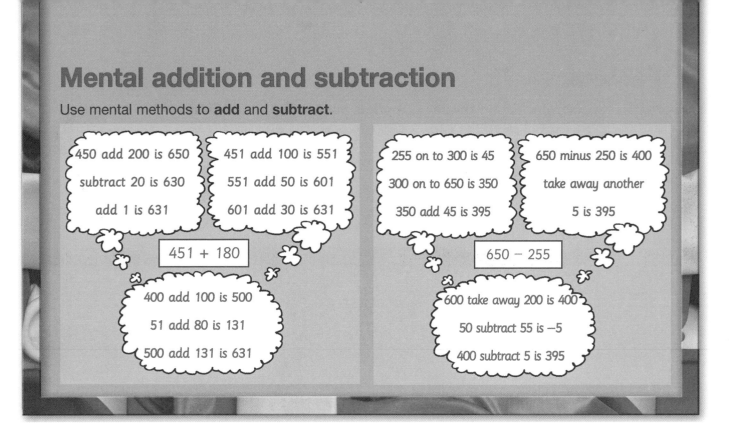

 Complete these addition squares. Add the rows and columns to find the totals.

a

67	84	151
92	45	137
159	129	288

b

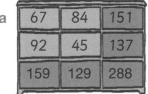

108	29	
76	52	

c

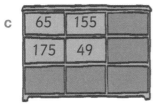

65	155	
175	49	

d

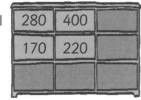

280	400	
170	220	

e

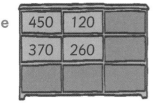

450	120	
370	260	

f

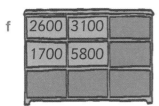

2600	3100	
1700	5800	

Work out the differences between these pairs of numbers.

g 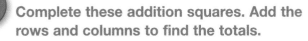 93   109

j  345   910

h 123   85

k 8100   8600

i 240   185

l 2400   7950

 5, 6 and 7 are consecutive numbers. Find three consecutive numbers to make each of these totals.

a ☐ + ☐ + ☐ = 57   **d** ☐ + ☐ + ☐ = 504

b ☐ + ☐ + ☐ = 81   **e** ☐ + ☐ + ☐ = 96

c ☐ + ☐ + ☐ = 339   **f** ☐ + ☐ + ☐ = 273

Factors

Factors are numbers that will **divide exactly** into other numbers.

Factors are often written in pairs.

Factors of 24

(1, 24)   (2, 12)   (3, 8)   (4, 6)

A **prime number** is a number with only two factors: 1 and itself.

7, 23, 29... are all prime numbers.

No other number divides exactly into these.

I Write the pairs of factors for these numbers.

a ⭐45   b ⭐18   c ⭐63   d ⭐30   e ⭐42   f ⭐40   g ⭐48

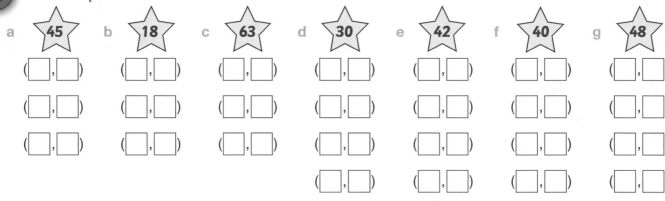

(☐ , ☐)   (☐ , ☐)   (☐ , ☐)   (☐ , ☐)   (☐ , ☐)   (☐ , ☐)   (☐ , ☐)

(☐ , ☐)   (☐ , ☐)   (☐ , ☐)   (☐ , ☐)   (☐ , ☐)   (☐ , ☐)   (☐ , ☐)

(☐ , ☐)   (☐ , ☐)   (☐ , ☐)   (☐ , ☐)   (☐ , ☐)   (☐ , ☐)   (☐ , ☐)

(☐ , ☐)   (☐ , ☐)   (☐ , ☐)   (☐ , ☐)

(☐ , ☐)

Write the factors for these square numbers in order.

h 25 ➜ [   ]   i 49 ➜ [   ]   j 64 ➜ [   ]

k What do you notice about the number of factors of square numbers?

_____

II Write the numbers 1 to 36 on this Venn diagram.

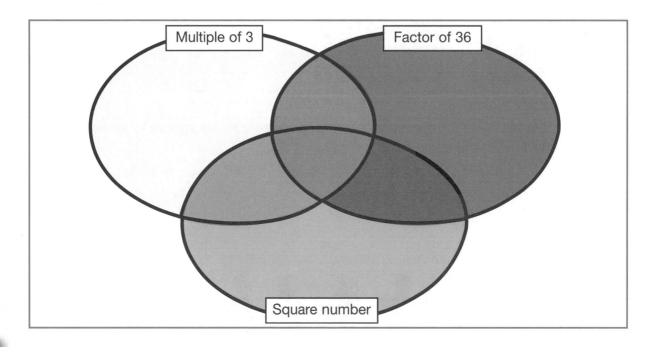

Multiple of 3   Factor of 36

Square number

Multiplication and division facts

To help learn division facts, use the related multiplication facts.

This trio makes the following facts:

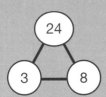

$3 \times 8 = 24$

$8 \times 3 = 24$

$24 \div 3 = 8$

$24 \div 8 = 3$

I Complete these.

a $9 \times 3 = \boxed{}$

$\boxed{} \div 3 = 9$

$\boxed{} \div 9 = 3$

c $4 \times 7 = \boxed{}$

$\boxed{} \div 4 = 7$

$\boxed{} \div 7 = 4$

e $6 \times 9 = \boxed{}$

$\boxed{} \div 6 = 9$

$\boxed{} \div 9 = 6$

b $7 \times 8 = \boxed{}$

$\boxed{} \div 8 = 7$

$\boxed{} \div 7 = 8$

d $8 \times 6 = \boxed{}$

$\boxed{} \div 8 = 6$

$\boxed{} \div 6 = 8$

f $5 \times 9 = \boxed{}$

$\boxed{} \div 5 = 9$

$\boxed{} \div 9 = 5$

Write the missing numbers for these multiplication grids.

g

x	7	8	4
6	42		
9			
		40	

h

x	6		5
	48		
			35
9		27	

i

x			
	56	42	21
	40	30	15
	72	54	27

 II Answer these as quickly as you can. Write the answers on a separate piece of paper, so you can try to beat your best time.

a $48 \div 6$

$90 \div 10$

$54 \div 9$

$64 \div 8$

$35 \div 5$

$36 \div 6$

b $18 \div 3$

$36 \div 4$

$27 \div 3$

$80 \div 8$

$32 \div 4$

$15 \div 5$

c $81 \div 9$

$45 \div 5$

$63 \div 7$

$49 \div 7$

$32 \div 8$

$16 \div 4$

d $72 \div 9$

$21 \div 3$

$60 \div 10$

$30 \div 5$

$48 \div 8$

$28 \div 4$

Fractions

In a fraction, the denominator shows how many parts an amount is divided into and the numerator shows how many of these parts to include.

$\dfrac{4}{5}$ → numerator
→ denominator

Equivalent fractions are worth the same.

$$\frac{4}{5} = \frac{12}{15}$$

To simplify fractions, use a factor of the **numerator** and **denominator** to divide.

$$\frac{12}{15} \div 3 = \frac{4}{5}$$

 Simplify these fractions.

a $\dfrac{6}{10} \div \square = \dfrac{\square}{\square}$

b $\dfrac{4}{12} \div \square = \dfrac{\square}{\square}$

c $\dfrac{10}{15} \div \square = \dfrac{\square}{\square}$

d $\dfrac{20}{24} \div \square = \dfrac{\square}{\square}$

e $\dfrac{30}{100} \div \square = \dfrac{\square}{\square}$

f $\dfrac{9}{24} \div \square = \dfrac{\square}{\square}$

g $\dfrac{18}{30} = \dfrac{\square}{\square}$

h $\dfrac{300}{500} = \dfrac{\square}{\square}$

i $\dfrac{18}{24} = \dfrac{\square}{\square}$

 Draw a line to join the matching pairs of fractions.

Addition

Before you add numbers, estimate an **approximate answer**.

If the numbers are too difficult to calculate mentally, you can use a written method.

17.8 + 29.6

↓

approximate answer

18 + 30

↓

48

```
   17.8
+  29.6
_____
   47.4
   ¹ ¹
```

Line up the decimal points and start adding from the right.

Estimate each answer, then calculate using a written method.

a estimate

```
   31.6
+  92.54
_____
```

c estimate

```
   46.51
+  39.74
_____
```

e estimate

```
   174.6
+   38.9
_____
```

g estimate

```
   358.2
+  147.9
_____
```

b estimate

```
    4.29
+  17.68
_____
```

d estimate

```
    3.07
+  68.19
_____
```

f estimate

```
   215.7
+  38.49
_____
```

h estimate

```
   491.6
+  87.95
_____
```

These vans can each carry a total of three crates. The total weight of the crates must be exactly 200 kg.

 80.59kg
 60.59kg
 85.17kg
 62.57kg
 76.84kg
 34.24kg

Which crates does each van take?

Van A

☐ kg + ☐ kg + ☐ kg = 200 kg

Van B

☐ kg + ☐ kg + ☐ kg = 200 kg

Time

To solve time problems, count on along a time line.

Count on from the start time to the finish in easy steps.

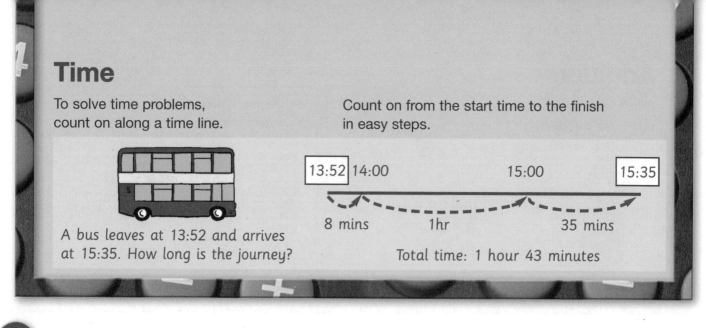

| 13:52 | 14:00 | | 15:00 | | 15:35 |

8 mins   1hr   35 mins

A bus leaves at 13:52 and arrives at 15:35. How long is the journey?

Total time: 1 hour 43 minutes

I   **Use the timetable to answer these questions.**

a What time does the 11:05 from Thorpe arrive in Salham?

_____

b How long does it take the 14:46 from Ashby to reach Welby?

_____

c What is the total journey time from Thorpe to Welby for train 4?

_____

d You arrive at Melton station for 2.50pm to catch a train to Salham. How many minutes will you wait for your train?

_____

e Which is the fastest train from Thorpe to Welby?

_____

f How long is the journey from Melton to Bilton on train 2?

_____

Timetable

Station	Train 1	Train 2	Train 3	Train 4
Thorpe	09:03	11:05	14:20	19:32
Ashby	09:28	11:31	14:46	19:59
Melton	09:50	12:02	15:15	20:30
Salham	10:13	12:27	15:39	20:53
Bilton	10:52	13:06	16:17	21:25
Welby	11:12	13:23	16:34	21:43

II   **Write your age in different ways. Remember leap years!**

☐ years (part year as a fraction)

☐ months

☐ weeks

☐ days

☐ hours

☐ minutes

☐ seconds

3-D shapes

Polyhedra are 3-D shapes made from a number of polygons. Each polyhedron has:

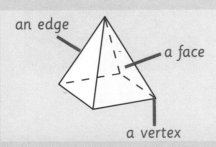

an edge

a face

a vertex

When a polyhedron is laid out flat, it makes the **net** of a shape.

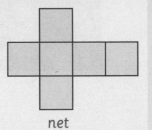

polyhedron

net

I Write the name of the shape that each net makes.

a

_____

c
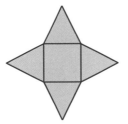
_____

e
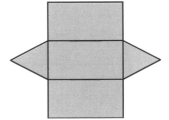
_____

b
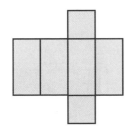
_____

d
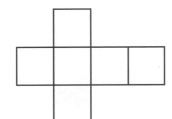
_____

f

_____

II Complete this chart.

Shape		Number of faces	Number of edges	Number of vertices
cube		6	12	8
cuboid				
tetrahedron				
square-based pyramid				
pentagonal prism				
triangular prism				

15

Area and perimeter

The area of a rectangle is length x width.

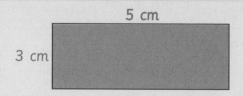

5 cm

3 cm

Area = 5 x 3 = 15 cm²

The perimeter of a rectangle is 2 x (length + width).

5 cm

3 cm

Perimeter = 5 + 5 + 3 + 3 = 16 cm

Some shapes can be split into rectangles.

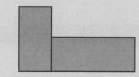

I Calculate the area and perimeter of each garden plan.

a
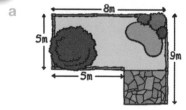
8m
5m
9m
5m

Area = ☐

Perimeter = ☐

c
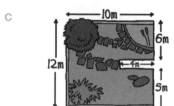
10m
6m
12m
4m
5m

Area = ☐

Perimeter = ☐

e
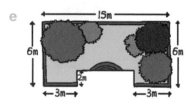
15m
6m
6m
2m
3m
3m

Area = ☐

Perimeter = ☐

b
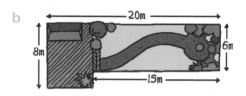
20m
8m
6m
15m

Area = ☐

Perimeter = ☐

d
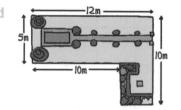
12m
5m
10m
10m

Area = ☐

Perimeter = ☐

f
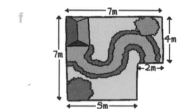
7m
4m
7m
2m
5m

Area = ☐

Perimeter = ☐

II Find the area of each part of this garden.

a Area of pond → ☐

b Area of paving → ☐

c Area of grass → ☐

d Area of whole garden → ☐

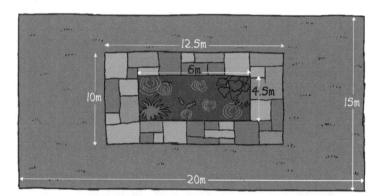

12.5m
6m
10m
4.5m
15m
20m

What is the area of this rectangle?

7 cm

3.2 cm

a 16 cm²

b 15.25 cm²

c 15.5 cm²

d 17 cm²

Answer: **none of them!!**

A crowd of 74 385 people watched a football match. What is this rounded to the nearest 100 people?

a 74 300   **c** 74 390

b 74 000   **d** 74 400

Answer: d

Which of these numbers has a remainder of 2 when it is divided by 9?

a 415   **b** 228   **c** 164   **d** 395

Answer: c

This is the net of which shape?

a cuboid

b tetrahedron

c square based pyramid

d triangular prism

Answer: b

In a maths test Ben scored 18 out of 20. What is this as a percentage?

a 98%   **b** 18%   **c** 90%   **d** 92%

Answer: c

What is the size of the missing angle?

50°   90°

a 40°

b 140°

c 220°

d 45°

Answer: a

Which of these is not a square number?

a 100   **b** 64   **c** 75   **d** 81

Answer: c

The area of a square is 144 cm². What is the length of each side?

a 11 cm   **c** 14 cm

b 12 cm   **d** 36 cm

Answer: b

Which of these numbers is a multiple of both 4 and 6?

a 90   **b** 72   **c** 86   **d** 92

Answer: b

What fraction is the same as 0.6?

a $\frac{3}{5}$ **b** $\frac{2}{3}$ **c** $\frac{1}{6}$ **d** $\frac{5}{6}$

Answer: a

Which of these fractions is not equivalent to $\frac{3}{5}$?

a $\frac{24}{40}$ **b** $\frac{30}{50}$ **c** $\frac{21}{30}$ **d** $\frac{300}{500}$

Answer: c

Which of these is a prime number?

a 15 **b** 11 **c** 27 **d** 21

Answer: b

What is the value of the circled digit?

3 9 . 0 ④ 7

a $\frac{4}{10}$ **b** 4 **c** 40 **d** $\frac{4}{100}$

Answer: d

What is the name for this quadrilateral?

a kite

b rhombus

c trapezium

d oblong

Answer: b

7.085 litres is the same as:

a 785 ml **b** 7850 ml

c 7085 ml **d** 708.5 ml

Answer: c

What is 38.4 multiplied by 100?

a 138.4 **c** 3814

b 384 **d** 3840

Answer: d

What is the answer to this?

$6 + (24 \div 3) = \square$

a 10 **b** 14 **c** 28 **d** 48

Answer: b

A train journey starts at 1745 and lasts for 2 hours 25 minutes. What time does it finish?

a 8.10pm **b** 10.10pm

c 9.55pm **d** 8.05pm

Answer: a

A full bucket holds 3.2 litres. A jug holds 0.4 litres. How many jugs are needed to half fill the bucket?

a 8   **b** 3   **c** 40   **d** 4

Answer: d

What is the value of y if:

$y + 6 = 12$?

a $y = 18$ **c** $y = 6$

b $y = 2$ **d** $y = 12$

Answer: c

What fraction of one hour is 20 minutes?

a $\frac{1}{20}$ **b** $\frac{1}{4}$ **c** $\frac{1}{6}$ **d** $\frac{1}{3}$

Answer: d

What is the remainder if 105 is divided by 8?

a 2   **b** 1   **c** 4   **d** 3

Answer: b

What is 25% of £300?

a £25   **b** £75   **c** £150   **d** £70

Answer: b

A birthday card costs £1.90. What change would there be from £10 for 4 cards?

a £3.40   **c** £2.60

b £2.40   **d** £2.80

Answer: b

What is the perimeter of this rectangle?

7.6 cm

2.4 cm

a 40 cm

b 19.64 cm

c 20 cm

d 17.6 cm

Answer: c

Which of these numbers is not a factor of 50?

a 4   **b** 2   **c** 5   **d** 25

Answer: a

What is 6.4 multiplied by 5?

a 50   **b** 32   **c** 34.5   **d** 30.2

Answer: b

What is the missing number?

−87   −78   ☐   −60   −51   −42

a −67   **b** −70   **c** −69   **d** −68

Answer: c

What is 10.36pm using 24-hour time?

a 1036   **b** 2036   **c** 1236   **d** 2236

Answer: d

Which of these numbers is not a factor of 63?

a 9   **b** 3   **c** 7   **d** 11

Answer: d

What is the missing number?

☐ ÷ 100 = 9.3

a 93   **b** 193   **c** 930   **d** 903

Answer: c

Which of these numbers is a multiple of both 4 and 9?

a 104   **b** 90   **c** 126   **d** 144

Answer: d

What is $\frac{3}{5}$ of £45?

a £15   **b** £24   **c** £12   **d** £27

Answer: d

What is the missing number?

0.45   0.41   0.37   ☐   0.29   0.25

a 0.33   **b** 0.32   **c** 0.3   **d** 0.34

Answer: a

What is the missing number?

1.8 + ☐ + 0.9 = 4.6

a 2.1   **b** 6.3   **c** 1.9   **d** 3.1

Answer: c

Which of these could be the missing number :

7.6 > ☐ > 7.45

a 7.39   **b** 7.65   **c** 7.51   **d** 7.42

Answer: c

Averages

Mean, **mode** and **median** are all different types of average.

Mode: the number that appears most often. <u>3</u> <u>3</u> 4 7 8

Median: the middle number when listed in order. 3 3 <u>4</u> 7 8

Mean: add the numbers and divide the total by the number of items used.

$$\frac{8 + 7 + 4 + 3 + 3}{5} = 5$$

 This graph shows the height of nine children. Look at it, then answer the questions.

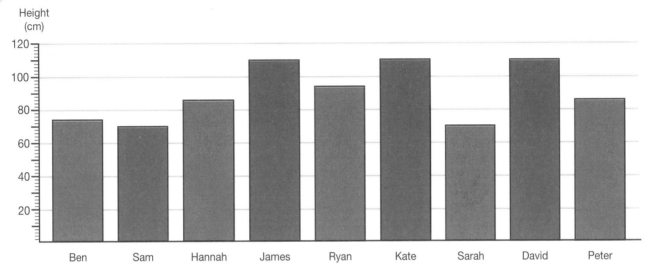

Height (cm) — bar chart with children: Ben, Sam, Hannah, James, Ryan, Kate, Sarah, David, Peter

a Write the heights in order, starting with the tallest child.

b What is the height mode? _____

c What is the median height? _____

d What is the mean height of all the children? _____

These are the shoe sizes for the nine children.

a Calculate the average shoe size for the children.

Mode → _____   Median → _____   Mean → _____

b What do you notice? _____

c Work out the average shoe size for your family or friends. _____

Symmetry

A line of symmetry is the same as a **mirror line**. One side of the line is the reflection of the other side.

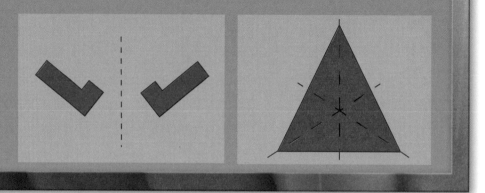

I **Draw the lines of symmetry on each shape.**

a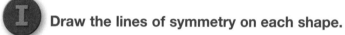

c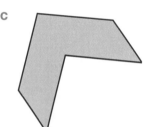

e

g

b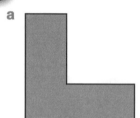

d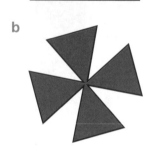

f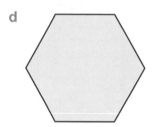

h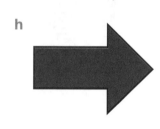

II **Draw the reflection of each shape.**

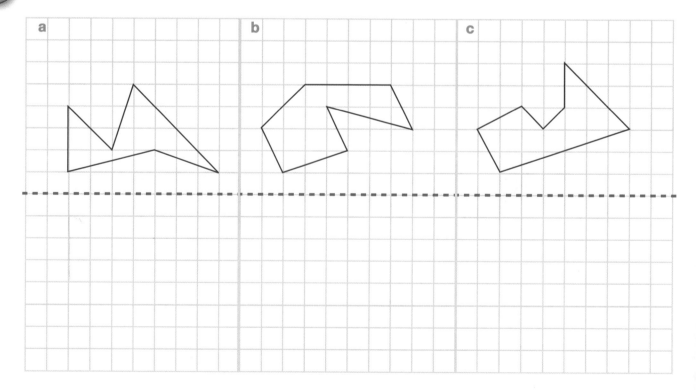

a   b   c

Measures problems

When you read a problem, try to 'picture' it in your head.

Think of the calculations that are needed to solve the problem.

Length	Mass	Capacity	
1 cm = 10 mm	1 kg = 1000 g	1 l = 1000 ml	250 g = $\frac{1}{4}$ kg
1 m = 100 cm	1 tonne = 1000 kg	1 cl = 10 ml	30 ml = 0.03 l
1 km = 1000 m			Use decimals and fractions to show parts.

 Answer these problems.

a Kelly travels 42.84 kilometres by car and 1350 metres on foot.

How far does she travel altogether in kilometres? _____

How far does she travel altogether in metres? _____

b A full bucket holds 2.8 litres. A jug holds 0.4 litres.

How many jugs will fill the bucket? _____

c A piece of wood is 27.68 metres long. Five equal lengths are cut
from the wood, leaving a length of 3.68 metres.
What is the length of each of the five pieces? _____

d A bus travels 15.8 kilometres in one journey. The bus does the journey six times a day
Monday to Friday and four times a day on Saturday and Sunday.

How many kilometres does the bus travel in total in one week? _____

 Look at the speed of these bugs, then answer the questions.

Anty travelled 25 cm in 10 seconds.

Bill travelled 1.3 m in 1 minute.

Cecil travelled 500 mm in 30 seconds.

Dennis travelled 1.5 cm in 1 second.

a Who was the fastest bug? _____

b Who was the slowest bug? _____

Ordering fractions

To compare the size of fractions, you can change them so they have the same, or common, denominator.

Example

Which is bigger $\frac{3}{5}$ or $\frac{2}{3}$?

Use equivalent fractions to find a common denominator.

$\frac{3}{5} = \frac{9}{15}$

$\frac{2}{3} = \frac{10}{15}$

So $\frac{2}{3}$ is bigger than $\frac{3}{5}$.

I Draw a circle around the fractions that are less than $\frac{1}{2}$. Colour the fractions that are less than $\frac{1}{4}$.

a $\frac{1}{3}$ c $\frac{1}{8}$ e $\frac{3}{5}$ g $\frac{5}{8}$ i $\frac{5}{9}$

b $\frac{5}{12}$ d $\frac{3}{10}$ f $\frac{7}{8}$ h $\frac{7}{10}$ j $\frac{3}{20}$

II Put each set of fractions in order, starting with the smallest.

a $\frac{1}{2}$ $\frac{1}{5}$ $\frac{3}{10}$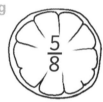

b  $\frac{2}{3}$ $\frac{3}{4}$ $\frac{7}{12}$

c $\frac{11}{12}$ $\frac{2}{3}$ $\frac{5}{6}$

d $\frac{7}{10}$ $\frac{11}{20}$ $\frac{4}{5}$

e $\frac{1}{3}$ $\frac{3}{8}$ $\frac{1}{4}$

f $\frac{5}{6}$ $\frac{7}{12}$ $\frac{1}{4}$

Handling data

Line graphs have points plotted that are joined with a line.

- Read up from the **horizontal axis** to meet the line or point.

- Read across to the **vertical axis** to give the value.

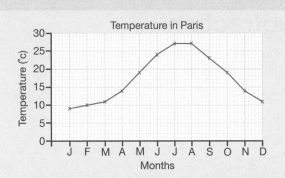

Temperature in Paris

I These are conversion graphs for pints and gallons. The conversions are approximate.

a Complete the line graph for gallons.

1 litre = 1.75 pints

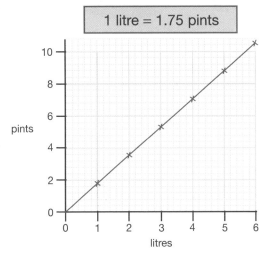

pints / litres

1 gallon = 4.5 litres

litres / gallons

Use the graphs to complete these.

b 8 pints = [　　] litres

c 5 litres = [　　] pints

d [　　] pints = 3.2 litres

e 2 gallons = [　　] litres

f [　　] litres = 3 gallons

g [　　] gallons = 22 litres

II Temperature is measured in degrees using two scales: Fahrenheit (°F) and Celsius (°C). This graph converts °F to °C approximately. Use the graph to complete this chart.

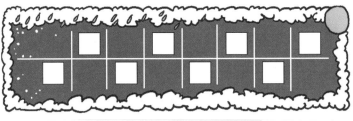

Graph to convert °F to °C

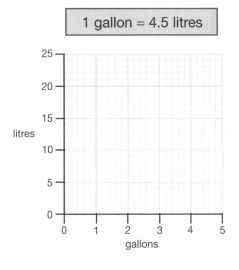

°C / °F

Subtraction

When you need to subtract decimal numbers, it may be too difficult to work out the answer mentally.

74.83 – 39.16

Estimate an approximate answer first. 75 – 40 = 35

Try this written method.

$$\begin{array}{r} {}^{6}\cancel{7}{}^{1}4 \,.\, {}^{7}\cancel{8}{}^{1}3 \\ -\ 39\,.\,16 \\ \hline 35\,.\,67 \\ \hline \end{array}$$

Start from the right-hand column.

Take away the bottom number from the top.

If the top number is smaller, exchange a ten.

I **Estimate and calculate each answer.**

a estimate

```
  17.85
-  9.93
```

c estimate

```
  73.92
- 27.18
```

e estimate
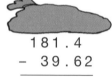

```
  181.4
- 39.62
```

g estimate
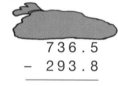

```
  736.5
- 293.8
```

b estimate

```
  34.16
-  8.77
```

d estimate
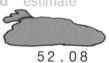

```
  52.08
- 16.14
```

f estimate

```
  372.1
- 87.93
```

h estimate
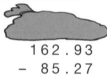

```
  162.93
-  85.27
```

II **Write the missing digits 0–9 in the spaces.**

a
```
  3 □ 1 . 6 9
-   5 8 . 7 4
-------------
  2 7 □ . 9 □
```

b
```
   2 7 □ . 9
- 1 □ 6 . 7 1
-------------
  1 6 5 . 1 9
```

c
```
  1 0 □ . 9
-   □ 8 . 7
-----------
   1 8 . 2
```

d
```
  □ 6 4 . 8 2
- 2 1 5 . □
-------------
  2 4 □ . 1 2
```

Percentages

Percent means 'out of 100'. The sign is %.

Percentages are fractions out of 100.

To change scores to percentages, make them out of 100.

8 out of 10 = $\frac{8}{10}$ = $\frac{80}{100}$ = 80%

10% of £12 → $\frac{1}{10}$ of £12 = £1.20

20% of £12 → double 10% = £2.40

5% of £12 → half 10% = 60p

I Change these test scores to percentages.

a 6 out of 10 = ☐ %

b 15 out of 20 = ☐ %

c 18 out of 20 = ☐ %

d 21 out of 25 = ☐ %

e 2 out of 10 = ☐ %

f 24 out of 25 = ☐ %

g 30 out of 50 = ☐ %

h 14 out of 25 = ☐ %

i 9 out of 20 = ☐ %

Write these percentages as fractions.

j 20% = $\frac{☐}{5}$

k 90% = $\frac{☐}{10}$

l 75% = $\frac{☐}{4}$

m 60% = $\frac{☐}{5}$

n 25% = $\frac{☐}{4}$

o 12% = $\frac{☐}{25}$

p 45% = $\frac{☐}{20}$

q 98% = $\frac{☐}{50}$

II Calculate these.

a 20% of 80 cm = ☐ cm

b 10% of £2.50 = ☐ p

c 25% of 400 ml = ☐ ml

d 5% of 80 kg = ☐ kg

e 20% of £12.50 = £ ☐

f 25% of 3.2 m = ☐ m

g 30% of 200 cm = ☐ cm

h 60% of 40 l = ☐ l

Approximation and rounding

When you round to the nearest 10, 100 or 1000, the halfway position is important.

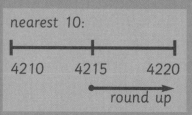

nearest 10:

4210   4215   4220

round up

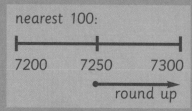

nearest 100:

7200   7250   7300

round up

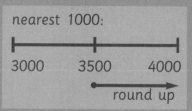

nearest 1000:

3000   3500   4000

round up

Numbers that are halfway or beyond are **rounded up**. The rest are **rounded down**.

I Round **these numbers.**

		to the nearest 10	to the nearest 100	to the nearest 1000
a	43 179 →			
b	789 155 →			
c	261 004 →			
d	749 968 →			
e	415 584 →			
f	29 465 →			
g	414 563 →			
h	254 564 →			

II Round **these to work out approximate answers.**

a

DAILY NEWS

The music festival had record crowds. 68,759 people went on Saturday, with 79,839 people on Sunday.

This is an approximate total of _____.

b

DAILY NEWS

The ancient woods were in a rectangular shape 978 metres long and 214 metres wide.

The approximate area of the woods is _____ m².

c

DAILY NEWS

The shopping centre had 211,482 visitors last month and 294,182 visitors this month.

This is an increase of approximately _____ visitors.

Equations

Equations have symbols or letters instead of numbers. You need to work out the missing numbers.

$x + 3 = 8$	$3n = 12$	$\frac{y}{2} = 8$
Use subtraction to help.	This means $n \times 3$.	This means $y \div 2$.
$8 - 3 = 5$ so $5 + 3 = 8$	Use division $12 \div 3 = 4$ so $3 \times 4 = 12$	Use multiplication $8 \times 2 = 16$ so $16 \div 2 = 8$
$x = 5$	$n = 4$	$y = 16$

  Work out the value of each letter.

a $4 + y = 9$

$y = $ ☐

b $a - 5 = 7$

$a = $ ☐

c $4c = 20$

$c = $ ☐

d $x + 8 = 15$

$x = $ ☐

e $\frac{x}{4} = 6$

$x = $ ☐

f $12 - y = 8$

$y = $ ☐

g $5n = 30$

$n = $ ☐

h $18 + y = 30$

$y = $ ☐

i $\frac{a}{6} = 3$

$a = $ ☐

Work out the value of each letter. These are tricky, so show your working out.

a $2x + 4 = 10$

$x = $ ☐

c $5a - 15 = 10$

$a = $ ☐

e $3x - 5 = 13$

$x = $ ☐

b $18 - 3y = 3$

$y = $ ☐

d $4c + 1 = 9$

$c = $ ☐

f $5 + 2a = 11$

$a = $ ☐

Fractions of amounts

To find a fraction of an amount, divide by the denominator.

$$\frac{1}{4} \text{ of } 24 = 24 \div 4 = 6$$

$$\frac{3}{4} \begin{array}{l} \leftarrow \text{ numerator} \\ \leftarrow \text{ denominator} \end{array}$$

When the numerator is more than 1, divide by the denominator and multiply by the numerator:

$$\frac{1}{4} \text{ of } 24 = 6$$

$$\frac{3}{4} \text{ of } 24 = 6 \times 3 = 18$$

I Answer these.

a What is $\frac{3}{5}$ of:

40 → ☐

25 → ☐

15 → ☐

100 → ☐

b What is $\frac{3}{4}$ of:

20 → ☐

12 → ☐

40 → ☐

100 → ☐

c What is $\frac{2}{3}$ of:

21 → ☐

9 → ☐

18 → ☐

33 → ☐

d $\frac{7}{8}$ of 800 ml = ☐ ml

e $\frac{2}{5}$ of 1000 g – ☐ g

f $\frac{2}{3}$ of 90 cm = ☐ cm

g $\frac{9}{10}$ of 70 kg = ☐ kg

h $\frac{3}{8}$ of 72 km = ☐ km

i $\frac{5}{6}$ of 180 l = ☐ l

II Answer these.

a What fraction of 1 year is 1 week? ☐

b What fraction of 1 hour is 45 minutes? ☐

c What fraction of 1 metre is 700 centimetres? ☐

d What fraction of £8 is 25p? ☐

e What fraction of 1 day is 8 hours? ☐

f What fraction of 1 year is 4 weeks? ☐

g What fraction of 1 minute is 20 seconds? ☐

h What fraction of £12 is 50p? ☐

Angles

Learn these rules for working out angles.

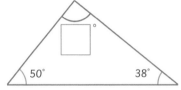

62° 118°

Angles in a straight line equal 180°.

90° 55° 35°

Angles of a triangle add up to 180°.

290° 70°

Angles at a point equal 360°.

I Work out the size of the missing angles.

a
105° ☐°

b
38° ☐°

c
☐° 97°

d
265° ☐°

e
☐° 97°

f
250° ☐°

g
☐° 50° 38°

h
49° 85° ☐°

i
☐° 115° 26°

II Work out these missing angles.

a
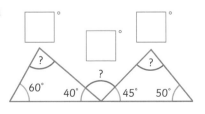
☐° ☐° ☐°
? ? ?
60° 40° 45° 50°

b
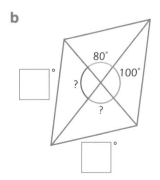
80° 100° ? ? ☐° ☐°

c
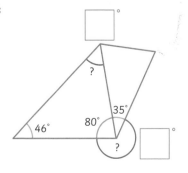
☐° ? 35° 46° 80° ? ☐°

27

Word problems

When you read a word problem, try to 'picture' the problem.

Try these four steps.

1 Read the problem. What do you need to find out?

2 Sort out the calculation. There may be one or more parts to the question. What calculations are needed?

3 Work out the answer. Will you use a mental or written method?

4 Check back. Read the question again. Have you answered it fully?

 I Answer these word problems.

Grass seed	Lawnmower	Large pot	Spade	Hedge trimmer	Fork
£6.70	£94.75	£11.40	£9.23	£107.59	£8.38

a What is the cost of a spade, a fork and some grass seed? _____

b How much change from £100 would there be if you bought a lawnmower? _____

c What is the cost of two pots and a hedge trimmer? _____

d What would be the total cost of five packets of grass seed? _____

What change would there be from £50? _____

e What is the difference in price between the spade and fork? _____

II Answer these questions about a trip to a fairground.

PRICES

Dizzy Dipper	X-ray Ride	Super Spin	Giant	Mars Mission	Big Wheel
£1.90	£2.05	£1.80	£2.15	£1.35	£1.55

Each of these children went on two rides. Which two rides did they go on?

a Alex: £1.50 change from £5. _____

b Harry: £6.30 change from £10. _____

c Rebecca: 15p change from £4. _____

d Emma: £5.95 change from £10. _____

e Which of these rides is the mean average price for the six rides? _____

Multiplication

There are different ways to work out multiplication calculations.

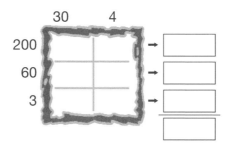

	20	7
300	6000	2100	→ 8100
384 x 27 → 80	1600	560	→ 2160
4	80	28	→ + 108

384 x 27 →

```
      6000    2100   →    8100
      1600     560   →    2160
        80      28   →  +  108
                        10 368
```

```
      384
  x    27
    7680
    2688
   10 368
```

384 × 27
is approximately
400 × 30
↓
12 000

I Answer these.

a 194 × 28

```
      20    8
100 [        ] → [    ]
 90 [        ] → [    ]
  4 [        ] → [    ]
                 [    ]
```

b 263 × 34

```
      30    4
200 [        ] → [    ]
 60 [        ] → [    ]
  3 [        ] → [    ]
                 [    ]
```

c 382 × 36

```
      30    6
300 [        ] → [    ]
 80 [        ] → [    ]
  2 [        ] → [    ]
                 [    ]
```

d
```
      2 3 5
  ×      3 1
  _____

  _____

  _____
```

e
```
      4 1 9
  ×      2 8
  _____

  _____

  _____
```

f
```
      3 2 7
  ×      4 3
  _____

  _____

  _____
```

II The volume of a cuboid is length × width × height. Calculate the volume of these cuboids.

a
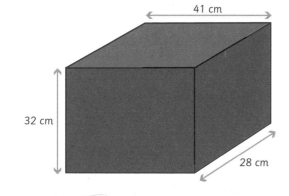

41 cm
32 cm
28 cm

Volume = _____ × _____ × _____

= [   ] cm³

b
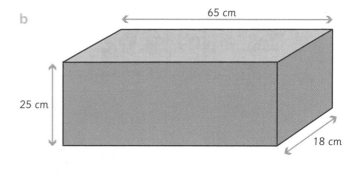

65 cm
25 cm
18 cm

Volume = _____ × _____ × _____

= [   ] cm³

Which cuboid has the greatest volume? _____

Division

A **quotient** is an answer to a division. Sometimes quotients can be decimal numbers.

Some decimal quotients go on and on as recurring decimals.

274 ÷ 5

```
      5 4 . 8
5 ) 2 7 4 . 0 0   ← add some zeros
      2     4
```
line up the decimal points

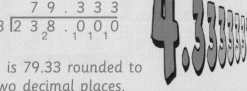

238 ÷ 3

```
      7 9 . 3 3 3
3 ) 2 3 8 . 0 0 0
      2   1 1 1
```

This is 79.33 rounded to two decimal places.

I Answer these using decimals.

a 5) 1 4 7

c 2) 7 4 7

e 8) 3 2 5

g 4) 6 4 9

b 4) 2 1 5

d 5) 4 1 8

f 2) 8 9 7

h 8) 4 7 1

Answer these, rounding the answer to two decimal places.

i 6) 1 7 5

k 7) 1 4 9

m 7) 3 0 9

o 3) 4 6 9

j 3) 2 5 0

l 9) 4 3 6

n 9) 6 4 7

p 6) 5 0 8

II All the 2s and 3s are missing. There are four of each number. Write them in the correct places.

a
```
      6 □ . □
5 ) □ 1 6
```

b
```
      7 □ . □ 5
8 ) 5 8 6
```

c
```
      1 □ 0 . 5
4 ) 5 □ □
```

Coordinates

Graphs have **axes**.

Axes are used to plot **coordinates**.

Position A is at (3, 2)

Position B is at (2, −4)

Position C is at (−2, 3)

Position D is at (−2, −2)

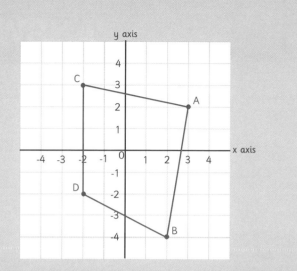

I **Draw these four triangles with the following coordinates.**

Triangle A

(2, 2) (4, 6) (7, 3)

Triangle B

(2, −2) (4, −6) (7, −3)

Triangle C

(−2, −2) (−4, −6) (−7, −3)

Triangle D

(−2, 2) (−4, 6) (−7, 3)

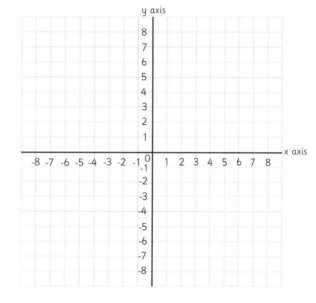

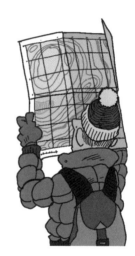

II **Plot these coordinates.**

(−4, 1)

(−8, 1)

(−5, 6)

(−1, 6)

Draw a reflection of this shape
and write the coordinates.

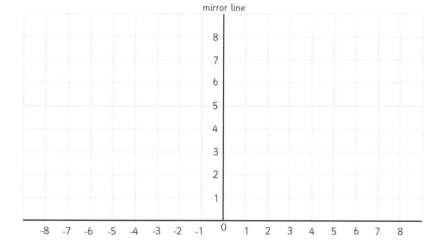

ANSWERS

Page 2

I a 74 500   **c** 48
561 000   273
865   49.1
29 800   621
311 400   380
2180   31.58
b 26 000   **d** 294
968 000   6148
6050   81.5
3   0.062
314 000   817
2 317 000   1722
19 800   13.1
1650   0.04

II a 100   **d** 6   **g** 100
    b 0.57   **e** 1000   **h** 160.5
    c 3.87   **f** 8500   **i** 94.13

Page 3

I a 23, 27, 31   Rule: +4
b −9, −17, −25   Rule: −8
c 13.5, 15, 16.5   Rule: +1.5
d 17, 50, 61
e 0.88, 0.87, 0.85
f 25, 10, −5
g 46, 55, 64
h 0.75, 1, 1.25
i −101, −82, −6

II a 25, 36, 49, 64
Rule: 1×1, 2×2, 3×3…etc.
They are square numbers.
b 15, 21, 28, 36
Rule: +2, +3, +4…etc
They are triangular numbers.
c 16, 32, 64, 128
Rule: Each number is double
the previous one.

Page 4

I a 3 tenths
b 6 thousandths
c 5 hundredths
d 8 tenths
e 6 hundredths
f 9 thousandths
g 1.99, 2.0
h 3.021, 3.022
i 4.95, 4.951
j 1.001, 1.002

II a 1.046   **c** 1.004
    b 1.247   **d** 1.058

Page 5

I a 930, 2004, 825, 726
b 296, 4120, 2004
c 2004
d 825, 930
e

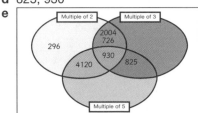

Page 6

I a 1:3
b 1:2
c 1:4
d a →16, b →24, c →12

II a Any 5 tiles red, any 15
tiles blue.
b Any 3 tiles green, any 12
tiles yellow.

Page 7

I a Quadrilateral, Square,
Rectangle, Rhombus,
Parallelogram, Trapezium, Kite
b Square, Rectangle, Rhombus,
Kite
c Square, Rectangle, Rhombus,
Parallelogram
d Square, Rhombus, Kite
e Square, Rectangle, Rhombus,
Parallelogram
f Square, Rectangle

II Check child's quadrilaterals.

Page 8

I a 6.05, 6.095, 6.198, 6.59,
6.625, 6.85, 6.9, 6.93
b 6.93   **c** 6.85   **d** 6.85
e Any of 6.05 6.095 6.198 6.59
or 6.625 **<6.82<** any of 6.85
6.9 or 6.93
f Any of 6.59 6.625 6.85 6.9 or
6.93 **>6.4>** any of 6.05 6.095
or 6.198
g Either 6.05 or 6.095 **<6.19<**
any of 6.198 6.59 6.625 6.85
6.9 6.93
II a Smallest – 1.269, 1.296, 1.629,
1.692, 1.926, 1.962
b Smallest – 9.126, 9.162, 9.216,
9.261, 9.612, 9.621

Page 9

I a

67	84	151
92	45	137
159	129	288

d

280	400	680
170	220	390
450	620	1070

b

108	29	137
176	52	128
184	81	265

e

450	120	570
370	260	630
820	380	1200

c

65	155	220
175	49	224
240	204	444

f

2600	3100	5700
1700	5800	7500
4300	8900	13200

g 16   **i** 55   **k** 500
h 38   **j** 565   **l** 5550

II a 18, 19, 20   **d** 167, 168, 169
    b 26, 27, 28   **e** 31, 32, 33
    c 112, 113, 114 **f** 90, 91, 92

Page 10

I a (1, 45) (3, 15) (5, 9)
b (1, 18) (2, 9) (3, 6)
c (1, 63) (3, 21) (7, 9)
d (1, 30) (2, 15) (3, 10) (5, 6)
e (1, 42) (2, 21) (3, 14) (6, 7)
f (1, 40) (2, 20) (4, 10) (5, 8)
g (1, 48) (2, 24) (3, 16) (4, 12) (6, 8)
h 1, 5, 25
i 1, 7, 49
j 1, 2, 4, 8, 64
k They have an odd number of
factors.

II

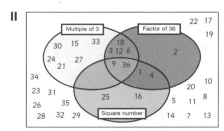

Page 11

I a 27, 27, 27   **d** 48, 48, 48
b 56, 56, 56   **e** 54, 54, 54
c 28, 28, 28   **f** 45, 45, 45

g

×	7	8	4
6	42	48	24
9	63	72	36
5	35	40	20

i

×	8	6	3
7	56	42	21
5	40	30	15
9	72	54	27

h

×	6	3	5
8	48	24	40
7	42	21	35
9	54	27	45

II a 8, 9, 6, 8, 7, 6
b 6, 9, 9, 10, 8, 3
c 9, 9, 9, 7, 4, 4
d 8, 7, 6, 6, 6, 7

Page 12

I a ÷2 = $\frac{3}{5}$ **f** ÷3 = $\frac{3}{8}$
b ÷4 = $\frac{1}{3}$ **g** $\frac{3}{5}$
c ÷5 = $\frac{2}{3}$ **h** $\frac{3}{5}$
d ÷4 = $\frac{5}{6}$ **i** $\frac{3}{4}$
e ÷10 = $\frac{3}{10}$

II

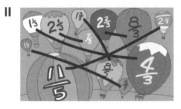

Page 13

I Estimates may vary slightly.
a estimate: 120   124.14
b estimate: 22   21.97
c estimate: 90   86.25
d estimate: 71   71.26
e estimate: 210   213.5
f estimate: 260   254.19
g estimate: 510   506.1
h estimate: 580   579.55

II Van A → 80.59 kg + 85.17 kg +
34.24 kg
Van B → 60.59 kg + 62.57 kg +
76.84 kg